W9-AGR-837

ESSAYS IN SKEPTICISM

ESSAYS
IN SKEPTICISM

by

BERTRAND RUSSELL

THE WISDOM LIBRARY

A Division of
THE PHILOSOPHICAL LIBRARY
New York

Distributed to the Trade
by BOOK SALES, INC.
New York

Copyright 1962 by Philosophical Library, Inc.,
15 East 40 Street, New York 16, N.Y.
By arrangement with Haldeman-Julius
Publications, Girard, Kansas.

Library of Congress Catalog Card No. 62-18547

Printed in the United States of America

Contents

I

MAN'S RECORD OF BELIEFS

PRINCIPAL CAUSES ARE HUMAN

The misfortunes of human beings may be divided into two classes: First, those inflicted by the non-human environment, and, second, those inflicted by other people. As mankind have progressed in knowledge and technique, the second class has become a continually increasing percentage of the total. In old times, famine, for example, was due to natural causes, and, although people did their best to combat it, large numbers of them died of starvation. At the present moment large parts of the world are faced with the threat of famine, but although natural causes have contributed to the situation, the principal causes are human. For six years the civilized nations of the world devoted all their best energies to killing each other, and they find it difficult suddenly to switch over to keeping each other alive. Having destroyed harvests, dismantled agricultural machinery, and disorganized shipping, they find it no easy matter to relieve the shortage of crops in one place by means of a super-abundance in another, as would easily be done if the economic system were in normal working order. As this illustration shows, it is now man that is man's worst enemy. Nature, it is true, still sees to it that we are mortal, but with the progress in medicine it will become more and more common for people to live until they have had their fill of life. We are supposed to wish to live forever and to look forward to the unending joys of heaven, of which, by miracle the monotony will never grow stale. But in fact, if you question any candid person who is no longer young, he is very likely to tell you that, having tasted life in this world, he has no wish to begin again as a "new boy" in another. For the future, therefore, it may be taken that much of the most important evils that mankind have to consider are those which they inflict upon each other through stupidity or malevolence or both.

MAN'S WORST ENEMY—MAN

I think that the evils that men inflict on each other, and by reflection upon themselves, have their main source in evil passions rather than in ideas or beliefs. But ideas and principles that do harm are, as a rule, though not always, cloaks for evil passions. In Lisbon when heretics were publicly burnt, it sometimes happened that one of them, by a particularly edifying recantation, would be granted the boon of being strangled before being put into the flames. This would make the spectators so furious that the authorities had great difficulty in preventing them from lynching the penitent and burning him on their own account. The spectacle of the writhing torments of the victims was, in fact, one of the principal pleasures to which the populace looked forward to enliven a somewhat drab existence. I cannot doubt that this pleasure greatly contributed to the general belief that the burning of heretics was a righteous act. The same sort of thing applies to war. People who are vigorous and brutal often find war enjoyable, provided that it is a victorious war and that there is not too much interference with rape and plunder. This is a great help in persuading people that wars are righteous. Dr. Arnold, the hero of "Tom Brown's Schooldays," and the admired reformer of Public Schools, came across some cranks who thought it a mistake to flog boys. Anyone reading his outburst of furious indignation against this opinion will be forced to the conclusion that he enjoyed inflicting floggings, and did not wish to be deprived of this pleasure.

OUR SADISTIC IMPULSES

It would be easy to multiply instances in support of the thesis that opinions which justify cruelty are inspired by cruel impulses. When we pass in review the opinions of former times which are now recognized as absurd, it will be found that nine times out of 10 they were such as to justify the infliction of suffering. Take, for instance, medical practice. When anesthetics were invented they were thought to be wicked as being an attempt to thwart God's will.

Insanity was thought to be due to diabolic possession, and it was believed that demons inhabiting a madman could be driven out by inflicting pain upon him, and so making them uncomfortable. In pursuit of this opinion, lunatics were treated for years on end with systematic and conscientious brutality. I cannot think of any instance of an erroneous medical treatment that was agreeable rather than disagreeable to the patient. Or again, take moral education. Consider how much brutality has been justified by the rhyme:

> A dog, a wife, and a walnut tree,
> The more you beat them the better they be.

I have no experience of the moral effect of flagellation on walnut trees, but no civilized person would now justify the rhyme as regards wives. The reformative effect of punishment is a belief that dies hard, chiefly I think, because it is so satisfying to our sadistic impulses.

But although passions have had more to do than beliefs with what is amiss in human life, yet beliefs, especially where they are ancient and systematic, and embodied in organizations, have a great power of delaying desirable changes of opinion and of influencing in the wrong direction people who otherwise would have no strong feelings either way. Since my subject is *"Ideas* That Have Harmed Mankind," it is especially harmful systems of beliefs that I shall consider.

THE PLACE OF RELIGION IN
MAN'S CRUEL RECORD

The most obvious case as regards past history is constituted by the beliefs which may be called religious or superstitious, according to one's personal bias. It was supposed that human sacrifice would improve the crops, at first for purely magical reasons, and then because the blood of victims was thought pleasing to the gods, who certainly were made in the image of their worshippers. We read in the Old Testament that it was a religious duty to exterminate conquered races completely, and that to spare even their cattle and sheep was an impiety. Dark terror and misfortunes in the life to come oppressed the Egyptians and Etruscans, but never reached their full development until the victory of Christianity. Gloomy saints who abstained from all pleasures of sense, who lived in solitude in the desert, denying themselves meat and wine and the society of women, were, nevertheless, not obliged to abstain from all pleasures. The pleasures of the mind were considered to be superior to those of the body, and a high place among the pleasures of the mind was assigned to the contemplation of the eternal tortures to which the pagans and heretics would hereafter be subjected. It is one of the drawbacks to asceticism that it sees no harm in pleasures other than those of sense, and yet, in fact, not only the best pleasures, but also the very worst, are purely mental. Consider the pleasures of Milton's Satan when he contemplates the harm that he could do to man. As Milton makes him say:

> The mind is its own place, and of itself
> Can make a hell of heaven, a heaven of hell.

and his psychology is not so very different from that of Tertullian, exulting in the thought that he will be able to look out from heaven at the sufferings of the damned. The ascetic depreciation of the pleasures of sense has not promoted kindliness or tolerance, or any of the other virtues that a non-superstitious outlook on human life would lead us to desire. On the contrary, when a man tortures himself he feels that it gives him a right to torture others, and inclines him to accept any system of dogma by which this right is fortified.

The ascetic form of cruelty is, unfortunately, not confined to the fiercer forms of Christian dogma, which are now seldom believed with their former ferocity. The world has produced new and menacing forms of the same psychological pattern. The Nazis in the days before they achieved power lived laborious lives, involving much sacrifice of ease and present pleasure in obedience to the belief in strenuousness and Nietzsche's maxim that one should make oneself hard. Even after they achieved power, the slogan "guns rather than butter" still involved a sacrifice of the pleasures of sense for the mental pleasures of prospective victory—the very pleasures, in fact, with which Milton's Satan consoles himself while tortured by the fires of hell. The same mentality is to be found among earnest Communists, to whom luxury is an evil, hard work the principal duty, and universal poverty the means to the millennium. The combination of asceticism and cruelty has not disappeared with the softening of Christian dogma, but has taken on new forms hostile to Christianity. There is still much of the same mentality; mankind are divided into saint and sinners; the saints are to achieve bliss in the Nazi or Communist heaven, while the sinners are to be liquidated, or to suffer such pains as human beings can inflict in concentration camps—inferior, of course, to those which Omnipotence was thought to inflict in hell, but the worst that human beings with their limited powers are able to achieve. There is still, for the saints, a hard period of probation followed by "the shout of them that triumph, the song of them that feast," as the Christian hymn says in describing the joys of heaven.

THE PSYCHOANALYSTS TAKE A LOOK

As this psychological pattern seems so persistent and so capable of clothing itself in completely new mantles of dogma, it must have its roots somewhat deep in human nature. This is the kind of matter that is studied by psychoanalysts, and while I am very far from subscribing to all their doctrines, I think that their general methods are important if we wish

7

to seek out the source of evil in our innermost depths. The twin conceptions of sin and vindictive punishment seem to be at the root of much that is most vigorous, both in religion and politics. I cannot believe, as some psychoanalysts do, that the feeling of sin is innate, though I believe it to be a product of very early infancy. I think that, if this feeling could be eradicated, the amount of cruelty in the world would be very greatly diminished. Given that we are all sinners and that we all deserve punishment, there is evidently much to be said for a system that causes the punishment to fall upon others than ourselves. Calvinists, by the fact of undeserved mercy, would go to heaven, and their feelings that sin deserved punishment would receive a merely vicarious satisfaction. Communists have a similar outlook. When we are born we do not choose whether we are to be born capitalists or proletarians, but if the latter we are among the elect, and if the former we are not. Without any choice on our own parts, by the working of economic-determinism, we are fated to be on the right side in the one case, and on the wrong side in the other. Marx's father became a Christian when Marx was a little boy, and some, at least, of the dogmas he must have then accepted seem to have borne fruit in his son's psychology.

EMOTIONS AND SUPERSTITION

One of the odd effects of the importance which each of us attaches to himself, is that we tend to imagine our own good or evil fortune to be the purpose of other people's actions. If you pass in a train a field containing grazing cows, you may sometimes see them running away in terror as the train passes. The cow, if it were a metaphysician, would argue: "Everything in my own desires and hopes and fears has reference to myself; hence by induction I conclude that everything in the universe has reference to myself. This noisy train, therefore, intends to do me either good or evil. I cannot suppose that it intends to do me good, since it comes in such a terrifying form, and therefore, as a prudent cow, I shall endeavor to escape from it." If you were to explain to this metaphysical ruminant that the train has no intention of leaving the rails, and is totally indifferent to the fate of the cow, the poor beast would be bewildered by anything so unnatural. The train that wishes her neither well nor ill would seem more cold and more abysmally horrifying than a train that wished her ill. Just this has happened with human beings. The course of nature brings them sometimes good fortune, sometimes evil. They cannot believe that this happens by accident. The cow, having known of a companion which had strayed on to the railway line and been killed by a train, would pursue her philosophical reflections, if she were endowed with that moderate degree of intelligence that characterizes most human beings, to the point of concluding that the unfortunate cow had been punished for sin by the god of the railway. She would be glad when his priests put fences along the line, and would warn younger and friskier cows never to avail themselves of accidental openings in the fence, since the wages of sin is death. By similar myths men have succeeded, without sacrificing their self-importance, in explaining many of the misfortunes to which they are subject. But sometimes misfortune befalls the wholly virtuous, and what are we to say in this case? We shall still be prevented by our feeling that we must be the center of the universe from admitting that misfortune has merely happened to us without anybody's intending it, and since we are not wicked by hypothesis, our misfortune must be due to somebody's malevolence, that is to say, to somebody wishing to injure us from mere hatred and not from the hope of any advantage to himself. It was this state of mind that gave rise to demonology, and the belief in witchcraft and black magic. The witch is a person who injures her neighbors from sheer hatred, not from any hope of gain. The belief in witchcraft, until about the middle of the 17th Century, afforded a most satisfying outlet for the delicious emotion of self-righteous cruelty. There was biblical warrant for the belief, since the Bible says: "Thou shalt not suffer a witch to live." And on this ground the Inquisition punished not only witches, but those who did not believe in the possibility of witchcraft, since to disbelieve it was heresy. Science, by giving some insight into natural causation, dissipated the belief in magic, but could not wholly dispel the fear and sense of insecurity that had given rise to it. In modern times, these same emotions find an outlet in fear of foreign nations, an outlet which, it must be confessed, requires not much in the way of superstitious support.

ENVY AS A SOURCE OF
FALSE BELIEFS

One of the most powerful sources of false belief is envy. In any small town you will find, if you question the comparatively well-to-do, that they all exaggerate their neighbors' incomes, which give them an opportunity to justify an accusation of meanness. The jealousies of women are proverbial among men, but in any large office you will find exactly the same kind of jealousies among male officials. When one of them secures promotion the others will say: "Humph! So-and-so knows how to make up to the big men. I could have risen quite as fast as he has if I had chosen to debase myself by using the sycophantic arts of which he is not ashamed. No doubt his work has a flashy brilliance, but it lacks solidity, and sooner or later the authorities will find out their mistake." So all the mediocre men will say if a really able man is allowed to rise as fast as his abilities deserve, and that is why there is a tendency to adopt the rule of seniority, which, since it has nothing to do with merit, does not give rise to the same envious discontent.

One of the most unfortunate results of our proneness to envy is that it has caused a complete misconception of economic self-interest, both individual and national. I will illustrate by a parable. There was once upon a time a medium-sized town containing a number of butchers, a number of bakers and so forth. One butcher, who was exceptionally energetic, decided that he would make much larger profits if all the other butchers were ruined and he became a monopolist. By systematically under-selling them he succeeded in his object, though his losses meanwhile had almost exhausted his command of capital and credit. At the same time an energetic baker had had the same idea and had pursued it to a similar successful conclusion. In every trade which lived by selling goods to consumers the same thing had happened. Each of the successful monopolists had a happy anticipation of making a fortune, but unfortunately the ruined butchers were no longer in the position to buy bread, and the ruined bakers were no longer in the position to buy meat. Their employes had had to be dismissed and had gone elsewhere. The consequence was that, although the butcher and the baker each had a monopoly, they sold less than they had done in the old days. They had forgotten that while a man may be injured by his competitors he is benefited by his customers, and that customers become more numerous when the general level of prosperity is increased. Envy had made them concentrate their attention upon competitors and forget altogether the aspect of their prosperity that depended upon customers.

THE FALSE PHILOSOPHY
OF ECONOMIC NATIONALISM

This is a fable, and the town of which I have been speaking never existed, but substitute for a town the world, and for individuals nations, and you will have a perfect picture of the economic policy universally pursued in the present day. Every nation is persuaded that its economic interest is opposed to that of every other nation, and that it must profit if other nations are reduced to destitution. During the first World War, I used to hear English people saying how immensely British trade would benefit from the destruction of German trade, which was to be one of the principal fruits of our victory. At the present time, although we should like to find a market on the Continent of Europe, and although the industrial life of Western Europe depends upon coal from the Ruhr, we cannot bring ourselves to allow the Ruhr coal industry to produce more than a tiny fraction of what it produced before the Germans were defeated. The whole philosophy of economic nationalism, which is now universal throughout the world, is based upon the false belief that the economic interest of one nation is necessarily opposed to that of another. This false belief, by producing international hatreds and rivalries, is a cause of war, and in this way tends to make itself true, since when war has once broken out the conflict of national interests becomes only too real. If you try to explain to someone, say, in the steel industry, that possibly prosperity in other countries might be advantageous to him, you will find it quite impossible to make him see the argument, because the only foreigners of whom he is vividly aware are his competitors in the steel industry. Other foreigners are shadowy beings in whom he has no emotional interest. This is the psychological root of economic nationalism, and war, and man-made starvation, and all the other evils which will bring our civilization to a disastrous and disgraceful end unless men can be induced to take a wider and less hysterical view of their mutual relations.

Another passion which gives rise to false beliefs that are politically harmful is pride—pride of nationality, race, sex, class, or creed. When I was young France was still regarded as the traditional enemy of England, and I gathered as an unquestionable truth that one Englishman could defeat three Frenchmen. When Germany became the enemy this belief was modified and English people ceased to mention derisively the French propensity for eating frogs. But in spite of governmental efforts, I think few Englishmen succeeded in genuinely regarding the French as their equals. Americans and Englishmen, when they become acquainted with the Balkans, feel an astonished contempt when they study the mutual enmities of Bulgarians and Serbs, or Hungarians and Rumanians. It is evident to them that these enmities are absurd and that the belief of each little nation in its own superiority has no objective basis. But most of them are quite unable to see that the national pride of a

Great Power is essentially as unjustifiable as that of a little Balkan country.

PRIDE OF RACE

Pride of race is even more harmful than national pride. When I was in China I was struck by the fact that cultivated Chinese were perhaps more highly civilized than other human beings that it has been my good fortune to meet. Nevertheless, I found numbers of gross and ignorant white men who despised even the best of the Chinese solely because their skins were yellow. In general, the British were more to blame in this than the Americans, but there were exceptions. I was once in the company of a Chinese scholar of vast learning, not only of the traditional Chinese kind, but also of the kind taught in Western universities, a man with a breadth of culture which I scarcely hoped to equal. He and I went together into a garage to hire a motor car. The garage proprietor was a bad type of American, who treated my Chinese friend like dirt, contemptuously accused him of being Japanese, and made my blood boil by his ignorant malevolence. The similar attitude of the English in India, exacerbated by their political power, has been one of the main causes of the friction that has arisen in that country between the British and the educated Indians. The superiority of one race to another is hardly ever believed in for any good reason. Where the Japanese were victorious, they entertained a contempt for the white man, which was the counterpart of the contempt that the white man had felt for them while they were weak. Sometimes, however, the feeling of superiority has nothing to do with military prowess. The Greeks despised the barbarians, even at times when the barbarians surpassed them in warlike strength. The more enlightened among the Greeks held that slavery was justifiable so long as the masters were Greek and the slaves barbarian, but that otherwise it was contrary to nature. Jews had in antiquity, a quite peculiar belief in their own racial superiority; ever since Christianity became the religion of the State Gentiles have had an equally irrational belief in their superiority to Jews. Beliefs of this kind do infinite harm, and it should be, but is not, one of the aims of education to eradicate them. I spoke a moment ago about the attitude of superiority that Englishmen have permitted themselves in their dealings with the inhabitants of India, which was naturally resented in that country, but the caste system arose as a result of successive invasions by "superior" races from the North, and is every bit as objectionable as white arrogance.

THE SUPERSTITION OF MALE SUPERIORITY

The belief in the superiority of the male sex, which has now officially died out in Western nations, is a curious example of the sin of pride. There was, I think, never any reason to believe in any innate superiority of the male, except his superior muscle. I remember once going to a place where they kept a number of pedigree bulls, and what made a bull illustrious was the milk-giving qualities of his female ancestors. But if bulls had drawn up the pedigree they would have been very different. Nothing would have been said about the female ancestors, except that they were docile and virtuous, whereas the male ancestors would have been celebrated for their supremacy in battle. In the case of cattle we can take the disinterested view of the relative merits of the sexes, but in the case of our own species we find this more difficult. Male superiority in former days was easily demonstrated, because if a woman questioned her husband's he could beat her. From superiority in this respect others were thought to follow. Men were more reasonable than women, more inventive, less swayed by their emotions, and so on. Anatomists, until the women had the vote, developed a number of ingenious arguments from the study of the brain to show that men's intellectual capacities must be greater than women's. Each of these arguments in turn was proved to be fallacious, but it always gave place to another from which the same conclusion would follow. It used to be held that the male foetus acquires a soul after six weeks, but the female only after three months. This opinion also has been abandoned since women have had the vote. Thomas Aquinas states parenthetically, as something entirely obvious, that men are more rational than women. For my part, I see no evidence of this. Some few individuals have some slight glimmerings of rationality in some directions, but so far as my observations go, such glimmerings are no commoner among men than among women.

SOME BAD EFFECTS
OF MALE DOMINATION

Male domination has had some very unfortunate effects. It made the most intimate of human relations, that of marriage, one of master and slave, instead of one between equal partners. It made it unnecessary for a man to please a woman in order to acquire her as his wife, and thus confined the arts of courtship to irregular relations. By the seclusion which it forced upon respectable women it made them dull and uninteresting; The only women who could be interesting and adventurous were social outcasts. Owing to the dullness of respectable women, the most civilized men in the most civilized countries often became homosexual. Owing to the fact that there was no equality in marriage men became confirmed in domineering habits. All this has now more or less ended in civilized countries, but it will be a long time before either men or women learn to adapt their behavior completely to the new state of affairs. Emancipation always has at first bad effects; it leaves former superiors sore and former inferiors self-assertive. But it is to be hoped that time will bring adjustment in this matter as in others.

CLASS DISTINCTIONS

Another kind of superiority which is rapidly disappearing is that of class, which now survives only in Soviet Russia. In that country the son of a proletarian has advantages over the son of a bourgeois, but elsewhere such hereditary privileges are regarded as unjust. The disappearance of class distinctions is, however, far from complete. In America everybody is of opinion that he has no social superiors, since all men are equal, but he does not admit that he has no social inferiors, for, from the time of Jefferson onward, the doctrine that all men are equal applies only upwards, not downwards. There is on this subject a profound and widespread hypocrisy whenever people talk in general terms. What they really think and feel can be discovered by reading second-rate novels, where one finds it is a dreadful thing to be born on the wrong side of the tracks, and that there is as much fuss about a mésalliance as there used to be in a small German Court. So long as great inequalities of wealth survive it is not easy to see how this can be otherwise. In England, where snobbery is deeply ingrained, the equalization of incomes which has been brought about by the war has had a profound effect, and among the young the snobbery of their elders has begun to seem somewhat ridiculous. There is still a very large amount of regrettable snobbery in England, but it is connected more with education and manner of speech than with income or with social status in the old sense.

PRIDE OF CREED

Pride of creed is another variety of the same kind of feeling. When I had recently returned from China I lectured on that country to a number of women's clubs in America. There was always one elderly woman who appeared to be sleeping throughout the lecture, but at the end would ask me, somewhat portentously, why I had omitted to mention that the Chinese, being heathen, could of course have no virtues. I imagine that the Mormons of Salt Lake City must have had a similar attitude when non-Mormons were first admitted among them. Throughout the Middle Ages, Christians and Mohammedans were entirely persuaded of each other's wickedness and were incapable of doubting their own superiority.

All these are pleasant ways of feeling "grand." In order to be happy we require all kinds of supports to our self-esteem. We are human beings, therefore human beings are the purpose of creation. We are Americans, therefore America is God's own country. We are white, and therefore God cursed Ham and his descendants who were black. We are Protestants or Catholics, as the case may be, therefore Catholics and Protestants, as the case may be, are an abomination. We are male, and therefore women are unreasonable; or female, and therefore men are brutes. We are Easterners, and therefore the West is wild and woolly; or Westerners, and therefore the East is effete. We work with our brains, and therefore it is the educated classes that are important; or we work with our hands, and therefore manual labor alone gives dignity. Finally, and above all, we each have one merit which is entirely unique, we are Ourself. With these comforting reflections we go out to do battle with the world; without them our courage might fall. Without them, as things are, we should feel inferior because we have not learnt the sentiment of equality. If we could feel genuinely that we are the equals of our neighbors, neither their betters nor their inferiors, perhaps life would become less of a battle, and we should need less in the way of intoxicating myth to give us Dutch courage.

THE DELUSION OF DIVINE FAVOR

One of the most interesting and harmful delusions to which men and nations can be subjected, is that of imagining themselves special instruments of the Divine Will. We know that when the Israelites invaded the Promised Land it was they who were fulfilling the Divine Purpose, and not the Hittites, the Girgashites, the Amorites, the Canaanites, the Perizzites, the Hivites, or the Jebbusites. Perhaps if these others had written long history books the matter might have looked a little different. In fact, the Hittites did leave some inscriptions, from which you would never guess what abandoned wretches they were. It was discovered, "after the fact," that Rome was destined by the gods for the conquest of the world. Then came Islam with its fanatical belief that every soldier dying in battle for the True Faith went straight to a Paradise more attractive than that of the Christians, as houris are more attractive than harps. Cromwell was persuaded that he was the Divinely appointed instrument of justice for suppressing Catholics and malignants. Andrew Jackson was the agent of Manifest Destiny in freeing North America from the incubus of Sabbath-breaking Spaniards. In our day, the sword of the Lord has been put into the hands of the Marxists. Hegel thought that the Dialectic with fatalistic logic had given supremacy to Germany. "No," said Marx, "not to Germany, but to the Proletariat." This doctrine has kinship with the earlier doctrines of the Chosen People and Manifest Destiny. In its character of fatalism it has viewed the struggle of opponents as one against destiny, and argued that therefore the wise man would put himself on the winning side as quickly as possible. That is why this argument is such a useful one politically. The only objection to it is that it assumes a knowledge of the Divine purposes to which no rational man can lay claim, and that in the execution of them it justifies a ruthless cruelty which would be condemned if our program had a merely mundane origin. It is good to know that God is on our side, but a little confusing when you find the enemy equally convinced of the opposite. To quote the immortal lines of the poet during the first World War:

Gott strafe England, and God save the King.
God this, and God that and God the other thing.
"Good God," said God, "I've got my work cut out."

22

Belief in a Divine mission is one of the many forms of certainty that have afflicted the human race. I think perhaps one of the wisest things ever said was when Cromwell said to the Scotch before the battle of Dunbar: "I beseech you in the bowels of Christ, think it possible that you may be mistaken." But the Scotch did not, and so he had to defeat them in battle. It is a pity that Cromwell never addressed the same remark to himself. Most of the greatest evils that man has inflicted upon man have come through people feeling quite certain about something which, in fact, was false. To know the truth is more difficult than most men suppose, and to act with ruthless determination in the belief that truth is the monopoly of their party is to invite disaster. Long calculations that certain evil in the present is worth inflicting for the sake of some doubtful benefit in the future are always to be viewed with suspicion, for, as Shakespeare says: "What's to come is still unsure." Even the shrewdest men are apt to be wildly astray if they prophecy so much as 10 years ahead. Some people will consider this doctrine immoral, but after all it is the Gospel which says "take no thought for the morrow."

In public, as in private, life the important thing is tolerance and kindliness, without the presumption of a superhuman ability to read the future.

THE CHANCES ARE THAT OUR
IDEAS ARE WRONG

Instead of calling this essay "Ideas that have harmed mankind," I might perhaps have called it simply "Ideas have harmed mankind," for, seeing that the future cannot be foretold and that there is an almost endless variety of possible beliefs about it, the chance that any belief which a man may hold may be true is very slender. Whatever you think is going to happen 10 years hence, and unless it is something like the sun rising tomorrow that has nothing to do with human relations, you are almost sure to be wrong. I find this thought consoling when I remember some gloomy prophesies of which I myself have rashly been guilty.

But you will say: How is statesmanship possible except on the assumption that the future can be to some extent foretold? I admit that some degree of prevision is necessary, and I am not suggesting that we are completely ignorant. It is a fair prophecy that if you tell a man he is a knave and a fool he will not love you, and it is a fair prophecy that if you say the same thing to 70,000,000 people they will not love you. It is safe to assume that cut-throat competition will not produce a feeling of good fellowship between the competitors. It is highly probable that if two States equipped with modern armament face each other across a frontier, and if their leading statesmen devote themselves to mutual insults, the population of each side will in time become nervous, and that one side will attack for fear of the other doing so. It is safe to assume that a great modern war will not raise the level of prosperity even among the victors. Such generalizations are not difficult to know. What is difficult is to foresee in detail the long-run consequences of a concrete policy. Bismarck with extreme astuteness won three wars and unified Germany. The long-run result of his policy has been that Germany has suffered two colossal defeats. These resulted because he taught Germans to be indifferent to the interests of all countries except Germany, and generated an aggressive spirit which in the end united the world against his successors. Selfishness beyond a point, whether individual or national, is not wise. It might with luck succeed, but if it fails failure is terrible. Few men will run this risk unless they are supported by a theory, for it is only theory that makes men completely incautious.

WHAT SOCIAL SCIENCE CAN DO

Passing from the moral to the purely intellectual point of view, we have to ask ourselves what social science can do in the way of establishing such causal laws as should be a help to statesmen in making political decisions. Some things of real importance have begun to be known, for example, how to avoid slumps and large-scale unemployment such as afflicted the world after the first World War. It is also now generally known by those who have taken the trouble to look into the matter that only an international government can prevent war, and that civilization is hardly likely to survive more than one more great war, if that. But although these things are known, the knowledge is not effective; it has not penetrated to the great masses of men, and it is not strong enough to control sinister interests. There is, in fact, a great deal more social science than politicians are willing or able to apply. Some people attribute this failure to democracy, but it seems to me to be more marked in autocracy than anywhere else. Belief in democracy, however, like any other belief, may be carried to the point where it becomes fanatical, and therefore harmful. A democrat need not believe that the majority will always decide wisely; what he must believe is that the decision of the majority, whether wise or unwise, must be accepted until such time as the majority decides otherwise. And this he believes not from any mystic conception of the wisdom of the plain man, but as the best practical device for putting the reign of law in place of the reign of arbitrary force. Nor does the democrat necessarily believe that democracy is the best system always and everywhere. There are many nations which lack the self-restraint and political experience that are required for the success of parliamentary institutions, where the democrat, while he would wish them to acquire the necessary political education, will recognize that it is useless to thrust upon them prematurely a system which is almost certain to break down. In politics, as elsewhere, it does not do to deal in absolutes; what is good in one time and place may be bad in another, and what satisfies the political instincts of one nation may to another seem wholly futile. The general aim of the democrat is to substitute government by general assent for government by force, but this requires a population that has undergone a certain kind of training. Given a nation divided into two nearly equal portions which hate each other and long to fly at each other's throats, the portion which is just less than half will not submit tamely to the domination of the other portion, nor will the portion which is just more than half show, in the moment of victory, the kind of moderation which might heal the breach.

WHAT THE WORLD NEEDS

The world at the present day stands in need of two kinds of things. On the one hand organization— political organization for the elimination of wars, economic organization to enable men to work productively, especially in the countries that have been devastated by war, educational organization to generate a sane internationalism. On the other hand it needs certain moral qualities—the qualities which have been advocated by moralists for many ages, but hitherto with little success. The qualities most needed are charity and tolerance, not some form of fanatical faith such as is offered to us by the various rampant isms. I think these two aims, the organizational and the ethical, are closely interwoven: given either the other would soon follow. But, in effect, if the world is to move in the right direction it will have to move simultaneously in both respects. There will have to be a gradual lessening of the evil passions which are the natural aftermath of war, and a gradual increase of the organizations by means of which mankind can bring each other mutual help. There will have to be a realization at once intellectual and moral that we are all one family, and that the happiness of no one branch of this family can be built securely upon the ruin of another. At the present time, moral defects stand in the way of clear thinking, and muddled thinking encourages moral defects. Perhaps, though I scarcely dare hope it, the atom bomb will terrify mankind into sanity and tolerance. If this should happen we shall have reason to bless its inventors.

II

INTELLECTUAL RUBBISH

Man is a rational animal—so at least I have been told. Throughout a long life, I have looked diligently for evidence in favor of this statement, but so far I have not had the good fortune to come across it, though I have searched in many countries spread over three continents. On the contrary, I have seen the world plunging continually further into madness. I have seen great nations, formerly leaders of civilization, led astray by preachers of bombastic nonsense. I have seen cruelty, persecution, and superstition increasing by leaps and bounds, until we have almost reached the point where praise of rationality is held to mark a man as an old fogey regrettably surviving from a bygone age. All this is depressing, but gloom is a useless emotion. In order to escape from it, I have been driven to study the past with more attention than I had formerly given to it, and have found, as Erasmus found, that folly is perennial and yet the human race has survived. The follies of our own times are easier to bear when they are seen against the background of past follies. In what follows I shall mix the sillinesses of our day with those of former centuries. Perhaps the result may help in seeing our own times in perspective, and as not much worse than other ages that our ancestors lived through without ultimate disaster.

Aristotle, so far as I know, was the first man to

proclaim explicitly that man is a rational animal. His reason for this view was one which does not now seem very impressive; it was, that some people can do sums. He thought that there are three kinds of souls: the vegetable soul, possessed by all living things, both plants and animals, and concerned only with nourishment and growth; the animal soul, concerned with locomotion, and shared by man with the lower animals; and finally the rational soul, or intellect, which is the Divine mind, but in which men participate to a greater or less degree in proportion to their wisdom. It is in virtue of the intellect that man is a rational animal. The intellect is shown in various ways, but most emphatically by mastery of arithmetic. The Greek system of numerals was very bad, so that the multiplication table was quite difficult, and complicated calculations could only be made by very clever people. Now-a-days, however, calculating machines do sums better than even the cleverest people, yet no one contends that these useful instruments are immortal, or work by divine inspiration. As arithmetic has grown easier, it has come to be less respected. The consequence is that, though many philosophers continue to tell us what fine fellows we are, it is no longer on account of our arithmetical skill that they praise us.

Since the fashion of the age no longer allows us to point to calculating boys as evidence that man is rational and the soul, at least in part, immortal, let us look elsewhere. Where shall we look first? Shall we look among eminent statesmen, who have so triumphantly guided the world into its present condition? Or shall we choose the men of letters? Or the philosophers? All these have their claims, but I think we should begin with those whom all right-thinking people acknowledge to be the wisest as well as the best of men, namely the clergy. If *they* fail to be rational, what hope is there for us lesser mortals? And alas—though I say it with all due respect—there have been times when their wisdom has not been very obvious, and, strange to say, these were especially the times when the power of the clergy was greatest.

The Ages of Faith, which are praised by our neo-scholastics, were the time when the clergy had things all their own way. Daily life was full of miracles wrought by saints and wizardry perpetrated by devils and necromancers. Many thousands of witches were burnt at the stake. Men's sins were punished by pestilence and famine, by earthquake, flood, and fire. And yet, strange to say, they were even more sinful than they are now-a-days. Very little was known scientifically about the world. A few learned men remembered Greek proofs that the earth is round, but most people made fun of the notion that there are antipodes. To suppose that there are human beings at the antipodes was heresy. It was generally held (though modern Catholics take a milder view) that the immense majority of mankind are damned. Dangers were held to lurk at every turn. Devils would settle on the food that monks were about to eat, and would take possession of the bodies of incautious feeders who omitted to make the sign of the Cross before each mouthful. Old-fashioned people still say "bless you" when one sneezes, but they have forgotten the reason for the custom. The reason was that people were thought to sneeze out their souls, and before their souls could get back lurking demons were apt to enter the un-souled body; but if any one said "God bless you," the demons were frightened off.

Throughout the last 400 years, during which the growth of science had gradually shown men how to acquire knowledge of the ways of nature and mastery over natural forces, the clergy have fought a losing battle against science, in astronomy and geology, in anatomy and physiology, in biology and psychology and sociology. Ousted from one position, they have taken up another. After being worsted in astronomy, they did their best to prevent the rise of geology; they fought against Darwin in biology, and at the present time they fight against scientific theories of psychology and education. At each stage, they try to make the public forget their earlier obscurantism, in order that their present obscurantism may not be recognized for what it is. Let us note a few instances of irrationality among the clergy since the rise of science, and then inquire whether the rest of mankind are any better.

When Benjamin Franklin invented the lightning-rod, the clergy, both in England and America, with the enthusiastic support of George III, condemned it as an impious attempt to defeat the will of God. For, as all right-thinking people were aware, lightning is sent by God to punish impiety or some other grave sin—the virtuous are never struck by lightning. Therefore if God wants to strike any one, Benjamin Franklin ought not to defeat His design; indeed, to do so is helping criminals to escape. But God was equal to the occasion, if we are to believe the eminent Dr. Price, one of the leading divines of Boston. Lightning having been rendered ineffectual by the "iron points invented by the sagacious Dr. Franklin," Massachusetts was shaken by earthquakes, which Dr. Price perceived to be due to God's wrath at the "iron points." In a sermon on the subject he said, "In Boston are more erected than elsewhere in New England, and Boston seems to be more dreadfully shaken. Oh! there is no getting out of the mighty hand of God." Apparently, however, Providence gave up all hope of curing Boston of its wickedness, for, though lightning-rods became more and more common, earthquakes in Massachusetts have remained rare. Nevertheless, Dr. Price's point of view, or something very like it, is still held by one of the most influential of living men. When, at one time, there were several bad earthquakes in India, Mahatma Gandhi solemnly warned his compatriots that these disasters had been sent as a punishment for their sins.

Even in my own native island this point of view still exists. During the last war, the British Government did much to stimulate the production of food at home. In 1916, when things were not going well, a Scottish clergyman wrote to the newspapers to say that military failure was due to the fact that, with government sanction, potatoes had been planted on the Sabbath. However, disaster was averted, owing to the fact that the Germans disobeyed *all* the Ten Commandments, and not only one of them.

Sometimes, if pious men are to be believed, God's mercies are curiously selective. Toplady, the author of "Rock of Ages," moved from one vicarage to another; a week after the move, the vicarage he had formerly occupied burnt down, with great loss to the new vicar. Thereupon Toplady thanked God; but what the new vicar did is not known. Borrow, in his "Bible in Spain," records how without mishap he crossed a mountain pass infested by bandits. The next party to cross, however, were set upon, robbed, and some of them murdered; when Borrow heard of this, he, like Toplady, thanked God.

Although we are taught the Copernican astronomy in our textbooks, it has not yet penetrated to our religion or our morals, and has not even succeeded in destroying belief in astrology. People still think that the Divine Plan has special reference to human beings, and that a special Providence not only looks after the good, but also punishes the wicked. I am sometimes shocked by the blasphemies of those who think themselves pious—for instance, the nuns who never take a bath without wearing a bathrobe all the time. When asked why, since no man can see them, they reply: "Oh, but you forget the good God." Apparently they conceive of the Deity as a Peeping Tom, whose omnipotence enables Him to see through bathroom walls, but who is foiled by bathrobes. This view strikes me as curious.

The whole conception of "Sin" is one which I find very puzzling, doubtless owing to my sinful nature. If "Sin" consisted in causing needless suffering, I could understand; but on the contrary, sin often consists in avoiding needless suffering. Some years ago, in the English House of Lords, a Bill was introduced to legalize euthanasia in cases of painful and incurable disease. The patient's consent was to be necessary, as well as several medical certificates. To me, in my simplicity, it would seem natural to require the patient's consent, but the late Archbishop of Canterbury, the English official expert on Sin, explained the erroneousness of such a view. The patient's consent turns euthanasia into suicide, and suicide is sin. Their Lordships listened to the voice of authority, and rejected the Bill. Consequently, to please the Archbishop—and his God, if he reports truly—victims of cancer still have to endure months of wholly useless agony, unless their doctors or nurses are sufficiently humane to risk a charge of murder. I find difficulty in the conception of a God who gets pleasure from contemplating such tortures; and if there were a God capable of such wanton cruelty, I should certainly not think Him worthy of worship. But that only proves how sunk I am in moral depravity.

I am equally puzzled by the things that are sin and by the things that are not. When the Society for the Prevention of Cruelty to Animals asked the Pope for his support, he refused it, on the ground that human beings owe no duty to the lower animals, and that ill-treating animals is not sinful. This is because animals have no souls. On the other hand, it is wicked to marry your deceased wife's sister—so at least the Church teaches— however much you and she may wish to marry. This is not because of any unhappiness that might result, but because of certain texts in the Bible.

The resurrection of the body, which is an article of the Apostles' Creed, is a dogma which has various curious consequences. There was an author not very many years ago, who had an ingenious method of calculating the date of the end of the world. He argued that there must be enough of the necessary ingredients of a human body to provide everybody with the requisites at the Last Day. By carefully calculating the available raw material, he decided that it would all have been used up by a certain date. When that date comes, the world must end, since otherwise the resurrection of the body would become impossible. Unfortunately I have forgotten what the date was, but I believe it is not very distant.

St. Thomas Aquinas, the official philosopher of the Catholic Church, discussed lengthily and seriously a very grave problem, which, I fear, modern theologians unduly neglect. He imagines a cannibal who has never eaten anything but human flesh, and whose father and mother before him had like propensities. Every particle of his body belongs rightfully to someone else. We cannot suppose that those who have been eaten by cannibals are to go short through all eternity. But, if not, what is left for the cannibal? How is he to be properly roasted in hell, if all his body is restored to its original owners? This is a puzzling question, as the Saint rightly perceives.

In this connection the orthodox have a curious objection to cremation, which seems to show an insufficient realization of God's omnipotence. It is thought that a body which has been burnt will be more difficult for Him to collect together again than one which has been put underground and transformed into worms. No doubt collecting the particles from the air and undoing the chemical work of combustion would be somewhat laborious, but it is surely blasphemous to suppose such a work impossible for the Deity. I conclude that the objection to cremation implies grave heresy. But I doubt whether my opinion will carry much weight with the orthodox.

It was only very slowly and reluctantly that the Church sanctioned the dissection of corpses in connection with the study of medicine. The pioneer in dissection was Vesalius, who was Court physician to the Emperor Charles V. His medical skill led the Emperor to protect him, but after the Emperor was dead he got into trouble. A corpse which he was dissecting was said to have shown signs of life under the knife, and he was accused of murder. The Inquisition was induced by King Philip II to take a lenient view, and only sentenced him to a pilgrimage to the Holy Land. On the way home he was shipwrecked and died of exhaustion. For centuries after this time, medical students at the Papal University in Rome were only allowed to operate on lay figures, from which the sexual parts were omitted.

The sacredness of corpses is a wide-spread belief. It was carried furthest by the Egyptians, among whom it led to the practice of mummification. It still exists in full force in China. A French surgeon, who was employed by the Chinese to teach Western medicine, relates that his demand for corpses to dissect was received with horror, but he was assured that he could have instead an unlimited supply of live criminals. His objection to this alternative was totally unintelligible to his Chinese employers.

Although there are many kinds of sin, seven of which are deadly, the most fruitful field for Satan's wiles is sex. The orthodox Catholic doctrine on this subject is to be found in St. Paul, St. Augustine, and St. Thomas Aquinas. It is best to be celibate, but those who have not the gift of continence may marry. Intercourse in marriage is not sin, provided it is motivated by desire for offspring. All intercourse outside marriage is sin, and so is intercourse within marriage if any measures are adopted to prevent conception. Interruption of pregnancy is sin, even if, in medical opinion, it is the only way of saving the mother's life; for medical opinion is fallible, and God can always save a life by miracle if He sees fit. (This view is embodied in the law of Connecticut.) Venereal disease is God's punishment for sin. It is true that, through a guilty husband, this punishment may fall on an innocent woman and her children, but this is a mysterious dispensation of Providence, which it would be impious to question. We must also not inquire why venereal disease was not divinely instituted until the time of Columbus. Since it is the appointed penalty for sin, all measures for its avoidance are also sin—except, of course, a virtuous life. Marriage is nominally indissoluble, but many people who seem to be married are not. In the case of influential Catholics, some ground for nullity can often be found, but for the poor there is no such outlet, except perhaps in cases of impotence. Persons who divorce and remarry are guilty of adultery in the sight of God.

The phrase "in the sight of God" puzzles me. One would suppose that God sees everything, but apparently this is a mistake. He does not see Reno, for you cannot be divorced in the sight of God. Registry offices are a doubtful point. I notice that respectable people, who would not call on anybody who lives in open sin, are quite willing to call on people who have had only a civil marriage; so apparently God does see registry offices.

Some eminent men think even the doctrine of the Catholic Church deplorably lax where sex is concerned. Tolstoy and Mahatma Gandhi, in their old age, laid it down that *all* sexual intercourse is wicked, even in marriage and with a view to offspring. The Manicheans thought likewise, relying upon men's native sinfulness to supply them with a continually fresh crop of disciples. This doctrine, however, is heretical, though it is equally heretical to maintain that marriage is as praiseworthy as celibacy. Tolstoy thinks tobacco almost as bad as sex; in one of his novels, a man who is contemplating murder smokes a cigarette first in order to generate the necessary homicidal fury. Tobacco, however, is not prohibited in the Scriptures, though, as Samuel Butler points out, St. Paul would no doubt have denounced it if he had known of it.

It is odd that neither the Church nor modern public opinion condemns petting, provided it stops short at a certain point. At what point sin begins is a matter as to which casuists differ. One eminently orthodox Catholic divine laid it down that a confessor may fondle a nun's breasts, provided he does it without evil intent. But I doubt whether modern authorities would agree with him on this point.

Modern morals are a mixture of two elements: on the one hand, rational precepts as to how to live together peaceably in a society, and on the other hand traditional taboos derived originally from some ancient superstition, but proximately from sacred books, Christian, Mohammedan, Hindu, or Buddhist. To some extent the two agree; the prohibition of murder and theft, for instance, is supported both by human reason and by Divine command. But the prohibition of pork or beef has only scriptural authority, and that only in certain religions. It is odd that modern men, who are aware of what science has done in the way of bringing new knowledge and altering the conditions of social life, should still be willing to accept the authority of texts embodying the outlook of very

40

ancient and very ignorant pastoral or agricultural tribes. It is discouraging that many of the precepts whose sacred character is thus uncritically acknowledged should be such as to inflict much wholly unnecessary misery. If men's kindly impulses were stronger, they would find some way of explaining that these precepts are not to be taken literally, any more than the command to "sell all that thou hast and give to the poor."

There are logical difficulties in the notion of Sin. We are told that Sin consists in disobedience to God's commands, but we are also told that God is omnipotent. If He is, nothing contrary to His will can occur; therefore when the sinner disobeys His commands, He must have intended this to happen. St. Augustine boldly accepts this view, and asserts that men are led to sin by a blindness with which God afflicts them. But most theologians, in modern times, have felt that, if God causes men to sin, it is not fair to send them to hell for what they cannot help. We are told that sin consists in acting contrary to God's will. This, however, does not get rid of the difficulty. Those who, like Spinoza, take God's omnipotence seriously, deduce that there can be no such thing as sin. This leads to frightful results. What! said Spinoza's contemporaries, was it not wicked of Nero to murder his mother? Was it not wicked of Adam to eat the apple? Is one action just as good as another? Spinoza wriggles, but does not find any satisfactory answer. *If* everything happens in accordance with God's will, God must have wanted Nero to murder his mother;

therefore, since God is good, the murder must have been a good thing. From this argument there is no escape.

On the other hand, those who are in earnest in thinking that sin is disobedience to God are compelled to say that God is not omnipotent. This gets out of all the logical puzzles, and is the view adopted by a certain school of liberal theologians. It has, however, its own difficulties. How are we to know what really is God's will? If the forces of evil have a certain share of power, they may deceive us into accepting as Scripture what is really their work. This was the view of the Gnostics, who thought that the Old Testament was the work of an evil spirit.

As soon as we abandon our own reason, and are content to rely upon authority, there is no end to our troubles. Whose authority? The Old Testament? The New Testament? The Koran? In practice, people choose the book considered sacred by the community in which they are born, and out of that book they choose the parts they like, ignoring the others. At one time, the most influential text in the Bible was: "Thou shalt not suffer a witch to live." Now-a-days, people pass over this text, in silence if possible; if not, with an apology. And so, even when we have a sacred book, we still choose as truth whatever suits our own prejudices. No Catholic, for instance, takes seriously the text which says that a Bishop should be the husband of one wife.

People's beliefs have various causes. One is that there is some evidence for the belief in question. We apply this to matters of fact, such as "what is so-and-so's telephone number" or "who won the World Series?" But as soon as it comes to anything more debatable, the causes of belief become less defensible. We believe, first and foremost, what makes us feel that we are fine fellows. Mr. Homo, if he has a good digestion and a sound income, thinks to himself how much more sensible he is than his neighbor so-and-so, who married a flighty wife and is always losing money. He thinks how superior his city is to the one 50 miles away: it has a bigger Chamber of Commerce and a more enterprising Rotary Club, and its mayor has never been in prison. He thinks how immeasurably his country surpasses all others. If he is an Englishman, he thinks of Shakespeare and Milton, or of Newton and Darwin, or of Nelson and Wellington, according to his temperament. If he is a Frenchman, he congratulates himself on the fact that for centuries France has led the world in culture, fashions, and cookery. If he is a Russian, he reflects that he belongs to the only nation which is truly international. If he is a Yugoslav, he boasts of his nation's pigs; if a native of the Principality of Monaco, he boasts of leading the world in the matter of gambling.

But these are not the only matters on which he has to congratulate himself. For is he not an individual of the species *homo sapiens?* Alone among animals he has an immortal soul, and is rational; he knows the difference between good and evil, and has learnt the multiplication table. Did not God make him in His own image? And was not everything created for man's convenience? The sun was made to light the day, and the moon to light the night—though the moon, by some oversight, only shines during half the nocturnal hours. The raw fruits of the earth were made for human sustenance. Even the white tails of rabbits, according to some theologians, have a purpose, namely to make it easier for sportsmen to shoot them. There are, it is true, some inconveniences: lions and tigers are too fierce, the summer is too hot, and the winter too cold. But these things only began after Adam ate the apple; before that, all animals were vegetarians, and the season was always spring. If only Adam had been content with peaches and nectarines, grapes and pears and pineapples, these blessings would still be ours.

Self-importance, individual or generic, is the source of most of our religious beliefs. Even Sin is a conception derived from self-importance. Borrow relates how he met a Welsh preacher who was always melancholy. By sympathetic questioning he was brought to confess the source of his sorrow: that at the age of seven he had committed the Sin against the Holy Ghost. "My dear fellow," said Borrow, "don't let that trouble you; I know dozens of people in like case. Do not imagine yourself cut off from the rest of mankind by this occurrence; if you inquire, you will find multitudes who suffer from the same misfortune." From that moment, the man was cured. He had enjoyed feeling singular, but there was no pleasure in being one of a herd of sinners. Most sinners are rather less egotistical; but theologians undoubtedly enjoy the feeling that Man is the special object of God's wrath, as well as of His love. After the Fall —so Milton assures us—

> The Sun
> Had first his precept so to move, so shine,
> As might affect the Earth with cold and heat
> Scarce tolerable, and from the North to call
> Decrepit Winter, from the South to bring
> Solstitial summer's heat.

However disagreeable the results may have been, Adam could hardly help feeling flattered that such vast astronomical phenomena should be brought about to teach *him* a lesson. The whole of theology, in regard to hell no less than to heaven, takes it for granted that Man is what is of most importance in the Universe of created beings. Since all theologians are men, this postulate has met with little opposition.

Since evolution became fashionable, the glorification of Man has taken a new form. We are told that evolution has been guided by one great Purpose: through the millions of years when there were only slime, or trilobites, throughout the ages of dinosaurs and giant ferns, of bees and wild flowers, God was preparing the Great Climax. At last, in the fulness of time, He produced Man, including such specimens as Nero and Caligula, Hitler and Mussolini, whose transcendent glory justified the long painful process. For my part, I find even eternal damnation less incredible, and certainly less ridiculous, than this lame and impotent conclusion which we are asked to admire as the supreme effort of Omnipotence. And if God is indeed omnipotent, why could He not have produced the glorious result without such a long and tedious prologue?

Apart from the question whether Man is really so glorious as the theologians of evolution say he is, there is the further difficulty that life on this planet is almost certainly temporary. The earth will grow cold, or the atmosphere will gradually fly off, or there will be an insufficiency of water, or, as Sir James Jeans genially prophesies, the sun will burst and all the planets will be turned into gas. Which of those will happen first, no one knows; but in any case the human race will ultimately die out. Of course, such an event is of little importance from the point of view of orthodox theology, since men are immortal, and will continue to exist in heaven and hell when none are left on earth. But in that case why bother about terrestrial developments? Those who lay stress on the gradual progress from the primitive slime to Man attach an importance to this mundane sphere which should make them shrink from the conclusion that all life on earth is only a brief interlude between the nebula and the eternal frost, or perhaps between one nebula and another. The importance of Man, which is the one indispensable dogma of the theologians, receives no support from a scientific view of the future of the solar system.

There are many other sources of false belief besides self-importance. One of these is love of the marvelous. I knew at one time a scientifically minded conjuror, who used to perform his tricks before a small audience, and then get them, each separately, to write down what they had seen happen. Almost always they wrote down something much more astonishing than the reality, and usually something which no conjuror could have achieved; yet they all thought they were reporting truly what they had seen with their own eyes. This sort of falsification is still more true of rumors. A tells B that last night he saw Mr. —, the eminent prohibitionist, slightly the worse for liquor; B tells C that A saw the good man reeling drunk, C tells D that he was picked up unconscious in the ditch, D tells E that he is well known to pass out every evening. Here, it is true, another motive comes in, namely malice. We like to think ill of our neighbors, and are prepared to believe the worst on very little evidence. But even where there is no such motive, what is marvelous is readily believed unless it goes against some strong prejudice. All history until the 18th Century is full of prodigies and wonders which modern historians ignore, not because they are less well attested than facts which the historians accept, but because modern taste among the learned prefers what science regards as probable. Shakespeare relates how on the night before Caesar was killed,

A common slave—you know him well by sight—
Held up his left hand, which did flame and burn
Like twenty torches join'd; and yet his hand,

47

Not sensible of fire, remain'd unscorch'd.
Besides—I have not since put up my sword—
Against the Capitol I met a lion,
Who glar'd upon me, and went surly by,
Without annoying me; and there were drawn
Upon a heap a hundred ghastly women,
Transformed with their fear, who swore they saw
Men all in fire walk up and down the streets.

Shakespeare did not invent these marvels; he found them in reputable historians, who are among those upon whom we depend for our knowledge concerning Julius Caesar. This sort of thing always used to happen at the death of a great man or the beginning of an important war. Even so recently as 1914 the "angels of Mons" encouraged the British troops. The evidence for such events is very seldom first-hand, and modern historians refuse to accept it—except, of course, where the event is one that has religious importance.

Every powerful emotion has its own myth-making tendency. When the emotion is peculiar to an individual, he is considered more or less mad if he gives credence to such myths as he has invented. But when an emotion is collective, as in war, there is no one to correct the myths that naturally arise. Consequently in all times of great collective excitement unfounded rumors obtain wide credence. In September, 1914, almost everybody in England believed that Russian troops had passed through England on the way to the Western Front. Everybody knew someone who had seen them, though no one had seen them himself.

This myth-making faculty is often allied with cruelty. Ever since the middle ages, the Jews have been accused of practicing ritual murder. There is not an iota of evidence for this accusation, and no sane person who has examined it believes it. Nevertheless it persists. I have met white Russians who were convinced of its truth, and among many Nazis it is accepted without question. Such myths give an excuse for the infliction of torture, and the unfounded belief in them is evidence of the unconscious desire to find some victim to persecute.

There was, until the end of the 18th Century, a theory that insanity is due to possession by devils. It was inferred that any pain suffered by the patient is also suffered by the devils, so that the best cure is to make the patient suffer so much that the devils will decide to abandon him. The insane, in accordance with this theory, were savagely beaten. This treatment was tried on King George III when he was mad, but without success. It is a curious and painful fact that almost all the completely futile treatments that have been believed in during the long history of medical folly have been such as caused acute suffering to the patient. When anesthetics were discovered, pious people considered them an attempt to evade the will of God. It was pointed out, however, that when God extracted Adam's rib He put him into a deep sleep. This proved that anesthetics are all right for *men*; women, however, ought to suffer, because of the curse of Eve. In the West votes for women proved this doctrine mistaken, but in Japan, to this day, women in childbirth are not allowed any alleviation through anesthetics. As the Japanese do not believe in Genesis, this piece of sadism must have some other justification.

The fallacies about "race" and "blood," which have always been popular, and which the Nazis have embodied in their official creed, have no objective justification; they are believed solely because they minister to self-esteem and to the impulse towards cruelty. In one form or another, these beliefs are as old as civilization; their forms change, but their essence remains. Herodotus tells how Cyrus was brought up by peasants, in complete ignorance of his royal blood; at the age of 12, his kingly bearing toward other peasant boys revealed the truth. This is a variant of an old story which is found in all Indo-European countries. Even quite modern people say that "blood will tell." It is no use for scientific physiologists to assure the world that there is no difference between the blood of a Negro and the blood of a white man. The American Red Cross, in obedience to popular prejudice, at first, when America became involved in the present war, decreed that no Negro blood should be used for blood transfusion. As a result of an agitation, it was conceded that Negro blood might be used, but only for Negro patients. Similarly, in Germany, the Aryan soldier who needs blood transfusion is carefully protected from the contamination of Jewish blood.

In the matter of race, there are different beliefs in

different societies. Where monarchy is firmly established, kings are of a higher race than their subjects. Until very recently, it was universally believed that men are congenitally more intelligent than women; even so enlightened a man as Spinoza decides against votes for women on this ground. Among white men, it is held that white men are by nature superior to men of other colors, and especially to black men; in Japan, on the contrary, it is thought that yellow is the best color. In Haiti, when they make statues of Christ and Satan, they make Christ black and Satan white. Aristotle and Plato considered Greeks so innately superior to barbarians that slavery is justified so long as the master is Greek and the slave barbarian. The Nazis and the American legislators who made the immigration laws consider the Nordics superior to Slavs or Latins or any other white men. But the Nazis, under the stress of war, have been led to the conclusion that there are hardly any true Nordics outside Germany; the Norwegians, except Quisling and his few followers, have been corrupted by intermixture with Finns and Laps and such. Thus politics are a clue to descent. The biologically pure Nordic loves Hitler, and if you do not love Hitler, that is proof of tainted blood.

All this is, of course, pure nonsense, known to be such by every one who has studied the subject. In schools in America, children of the most diverse origins are subjected to the same educational system, and those whose business it is to measure intelligence quotients and otherwise estimate the native ability of students are unable to make any such racial distinctions as are postulated by the theorists of race. In every national or racial group there are clever children and stupid children. It is not likely that, in the United States, colored children will develop as successfully as white children, because of the stigma of social inferiority; but in so far as congenital ability can be detached from environmental influence, there is no clear distinction among different groups. The whole conception of superior races is merely a myth generated by the overweening self-esteem of the holders of power. It may be that, some day, better evidence will be forthcoming; perhaps, in time, educators will be able to prove (say) that Jews are on the average more intelligent than gentiles. But as yet no such evidence exists, and all talk of superior races must be dismissed as nonsense.

There is a special absurdity in applying racial theories to the various populations of Europe. There is not in Europe any such thing as a pure race. Russians have an admixture of Tartar blood, Germans are largely Slavonic, France is a mixture of Celts, Germans, and people of Mediterranean race, Italy the same with the addition of the descendants of slaves imported by the Romans. The English are perhaps the most mixed of all. There is no evidence that there is any advantage in belonging to a pure race. The purest races now in existence are the Pygmies, the Hottentots, and the Australian aborigines; the Tasmanians, who were probably even purer, are extinct. They were not the bearers of a brilliant culture. The ancient Greeks, on the other hand, emerged from an amalgamation of northern barbarians and an indigenous population; the Athenians and Ionians, who were the most civilized, were also the most mixed. The supposed merits of racial purity are, it would seem, wholly imaginary.

Superstitions about blood have many forms that have nothing to do with race. The objection to homicide seems to have been, originally, based on the ritual pollution caused by the blood of the victim. God said to Cain: "The voice of thy brother's blood crieth unto me from the ground." According to some anthropologists, the mark of Cain was a disguise to prevent Abel's blood from finding him; this appears also to be the original reason for wearing mourning. In many ancient communities no difference was made between murder and accidental homicide; in either case equally ritual ablution was necessary. The feeling that blood defiles still lingers, for example in the Churching of Women and in tabus connected with menstruation. The idea that a child is of his father's "blood" has the same superstitious origin. So far as actual blood is concerned, the mother's enters into the child, but not the father's. If blood were as important as is supposed, matriarchy would be the only proper way of tracing descent.

In Russia, where, under the influence of Karl Marx, people since the revolution have been classified by their economic origin, difficulties have arisen not unlike those of German race theorists over the Scandinavian Nordics. There were two theories that had to be reconciled: on the one hand, proletarians were good and other people were bad; on the other hand, communists were good and other people were bad. The only way of effecting a reconciliation was to alter the meaning of words. A "proletarian" came to mean a supporter of the government; Lenin, though born a Prince, was reckoned a member of the proletariat. On the other hand, the word "kulak," which was supposed to mean a rich peasant, came to mean any peasant who opposed collectivization. This sort of absurdity always arises when one group of human beings is supposed to be inherently better than another. In America, the highest praise that can be bestowed on an eminent colored man after he is safely dead is to say "he was a *white* man." A courageous woman is called "masculine": Macbeth, praising his wife's courage, says:

> Bring forth men children only,
> For thy undaunted mettle should compose
> Nothing but males.

All these ways of speaking come of unwillingness to abandon foolish generalizations.

In the economic sphere there are many wide-spread superstitions.

Why do people value gold and precious stones? Not simply because of their rarity: there are a number of elements called "rare earths" which are much rarer than gold, but no one will give a penny for them except a few men of science. There is a theory, for which there is much to be said, that gold and gems were valued originally on account of their supposed magical properties. The mistakes of governments in modern times seem to show that this belief still exists among the sort of men who are called "practical." At the end of the last war, it was agreed that Germany should pay vast sums to England and France, and they in turn should pay vast sums to the United States. Every one wanted to be paid in money rather than goods; the "practical" men failed to notice that there is not that amount of money in the world. They also failed to notice that money is no use unless it is used to buy goods. As they would not use it in this way, it did no good to anyone. There was supposed to be some mystic virtue about gold that made it worth while to dig it up in the Transvaal and put it underground again in bank vaults in America. In the end, of course, the debtor countries had no more money, and, since they were not allowed to pay in goods, they went bankrupt. The great depression was the direct result of the surviving belief in the magical properties of gold. It is to be feared that some similar superstition will cause equally bad results after the end of the present war.

Politics is largely governed by sententious platitudes which are devoid of truth.

One of the most wide-spread popular maxims is, "human nature cannot be changed." No one can say whether this is true or not without first defining "human nature." But as used it is certainly false. When Mr. A. utters the maxim, with an air of portentous and conclusive wisdom, what he means is that all men everywhere will always continue to behave as they do in his own home town. A little anthropology will dispel this belief. Among the Tibetans, one wife has many husbands, because men are too poor to support a whole wife; yet family life, according to travelers, is no more unhappy than elsewhere. The practice of lending one's wife to a guest is very common among uncivilized tribes. The Australian aborigines, at puberty, undergo a very painful operation which, throughout the rest of their lives, greatly diminishes sexual potency. Infanticide, which might seem contrary to human nature, was almost univerversal before the rise of Christianity, and is recommended by Plato to prevent over-population. Private property is not recognized among some savage tribes. Even among highly civilized people, economic considerations will override what is called "human nature." In Moscow, where there is an acute housing shortage, when an unmarried woman is pregnant, it often happens that a number of men contend for the legal right to be considered the father of the prospective child, because whoever is judged to be the father acquires the right to share the woman's room, and half a room is better than no roof.

In fact, adult "human nature" is extremely variable, according to the circumstances of education. Food and sex are very general requirements, but the hermits of the Thebaid eschewed sex altogether and reduced food to the lowest point compatible with survival. By diet and training, people can be made ferocious or meek, masterful or slavish, as may suit the educator. There is no nonsense so arrant that it cannot be made the creed of the vast majority by adequate governmental action. Plato intended his Republic to be founded on a myth which he admitted to be absurd, but he was rightly confident that the populace could be induced to believe it. Hobbes, who thought it important that people should reverence the government however unworthy it might be, meets the argument that it might be difficult to obtain general assent to anything so irrational by pointing out that people have been brought to believe in the Christian religion, and, in particular, in the dogma of transubstantiation. If he had been alive now, he would have found ample confirmation of his contention in the devotion of German youth to the Nazis.

The power of governments over men's beliefs has been very great ever since the rise of large States. The great majority of Romans became Christian after the Roman Emperors had been converted. In the parts of the Roman Empire that were conquered by the Arabs, most people abandoned Christianity for Islam. The division of Western Europe into Protestant and Catholic regions was determined by the attitude of governments in the 16th Century. But the power of governments over belief in the present day is vastly greater than at any earlier time. A belief, however untrue, is important when it dominates the actions of large masses of men. In this sense, the beliefs inculcated by the Japanese, Russian, and German governments are important. Since they are completely divergent, they cannot all be true, though they may well all be false. Unfortunately they are such as to inspire men with an ardent desire to kill one another, even to the point of almost completely inhibiting the impulse of self-preservation. No one can deny, in face of the evidence, that it is easy, given military power, to produce a population of fanatical lunatics. It would be equally easy to produce a population of sane and reasonable people, but many governments do not wish to do so, since such people would fail to admire the politicians who are at the head of these governments.

There is one peculiarly pernicious application of the doctrine that human nature cannot be changed. This is the dogmatic assertion that there will always be wars, because we are so constituted that we feel a need of them. What is true is that a man who has had the kind of diet and education that most men have will wish to fight when provoked. But he will not actually fight unless he has a chance of victory. It is very annoying to be stopped by a speed cop, but we do not fight him because we know that he has the overwhelming forces of the State at his back. People who have no occasion for war do not make any impression of being psychologically thwarted. Sweden has had no war since 1814, but the Swedes were, a few years ago, one of the happiest and most contented nations in the world. I doubt whether they are so still, but that is because, though neutral, they are unable to escape many of the evils of war. If political organization were such as to make war obviously unprofitable, there is nothing in human nature that would compel its occurrence, or make average people unhappy because of its not occurring. Exactly the same arguments that are now used about the impossibility of preventing war were formerly used in defense of duelling, yet few of us feel thwarted because we are not allowed to fight duels.

I am persuaded that there is absolutely no limit to the absurdities that can, by government action, come to be generally believed. Give me an adequate army, with power to provide it with more pay and better food than falls to the lot of the average man, and I will undertake, within 30 years, to make the majority of the population believe that two and two are three, that water freezes when it gets hot and boils when it gets cold, or any other nonsense that might seem to serve the interest of the State. Of course, even when these beliefs had been generated, people would not put the kettle in the ice-box when they wanted it to boil. That cold makes water boil would be a Sunday truth, sacred and mystical, to be professed in awed tones, but not to be acted on in daily life. What would happen would be that any verbal denial of the mystic doctrine would be made illegal, and obstinate heretics would be "frozen" at the stake. No person who did not enthusiastically accept the official doctrine would be allowed to teach or to have any position of power. Only the very highest officials, in their cups, would whisper to each other what rubbish it all is; then they would laugh and drink again. This is hardly a caricature of what happens under some modern governments.

The discovery that man can be scientifically manipulated, and that governments can turn large masses this way or that as they choose, is one of the causes of our misfortunes. There is as much difference between a collection of mentally free citizens and a community moulded by modern methods of propaganda as there is between a heap of raw materials and a battleship. Education, which was at first made universal in order that all might be able to read and write, has been found capable of serving quite other purposes. By instilling nonsense it unifies populations and generates collective enthusiasm. If all governments taught the same nonsense, the harm would not be so great. Unfortunately each has its own brand, and the diversity serves to produce hostility between the devotees of different creeds. If there is ever to be peace in the world, governments will have to agree either to inculcate no dogmas, or all to inculcate the same. The former, I fear, is a Utopian ideal, but perhaps they would agree to teach collectively that all public men, everywhere, are completely virtuous and perfectly wise. Perhaps, when the war is over, the surviving politicians may find it prudent to combine on some such program.

But if conformity has its dangers, so has non-conformity.

Some "advanced thinkers" are of opinion that any one who differs from the conventional opinion must be in the right. This is a delusion; if it were not, truth would be easier to come by than it is. There are infinite possibilities of error, and more cranks take up unfashionable errors than unfashionable truths. I met once an electrical engineer whose first words to me were: "How do you do. There are two methods of faith-healing, the one practiced by Christ and the one practiced by most Christian Scientists. I practice the method practiced by Christ." Shortly afterwards, he was sent to prison for making out fraudulent balance-sheets. The law does not look kindly on the intrusion of faith into this region. I knew also an eminent lunacy doctor who took to philosophy, and taught a new logic which, as he frankly confessed, he had learnt from his lunatics. When he died, he left a will founding a professorship for the teaching of his new scientific methods, but unfortunately he left no assets. Arithmetic proved recalcitrant to lunatic logic. On one occasion a man came to ask me to recommend some of my books, as he was interested in philosophy. I did so, but he returned next day saying that he had been reading one of them, and had found only one statement he could understand, and that one seemed to him false. I asked him what it was, and he said it was the statement that Julius Caesar is dead. When I asked him why he did not agree, he drew himself up and said: "Because I am Julius Caesar." These examples may suffice to show that you cannot make sure of being right by being eccentric.

Science, which has always had to fight its way against popular beliefs, now has one of its most difficult battles in the sphere of psychology.

People who think they know all about human nature are always hopelessly at sea when they have to do with any abnormality. Some boys never learn to be what, in animals, is called "house-trained." The sort of person who won't stand any nonsense deals with such cases by punishment; the boy is beaten, and when he repeats the offense he is beaten worse. All medical men who have studied the matter know that punishment only aggravates the trouble. Sometimes the cause is physical, but usually it is psychological, and only curable by removing some deep-seated and probably unconscious grievance. But most people enjoy punishing anyone who irritates them, and so the medical view is rejected as fancy nonsense. The same sort of thing applies to men who are exhibitionists; they are sent to prison over and over again, but as soon as they come out they repeat the offense. A medical man who specialized in such ailments assured me that the exhibitionist can be cured by the simple device of having trousers that button up the back instead of the front. But this method is not tried because it does not satisfy people's vindictive impulses.

Broadly speaking, punishment is likely to prevent crimes that are sane in origin, but not those that spring from some psychological abnormality. This is now partially recognized; we distinguish between plain theft, which springs from what may be called rational self-interest, and kleptomania, which is a mark of something queer. And homicidal maniacs are not treated like ordinary murderers. But sexual aberrations rouse so much disgust that it is still impossible to have them treated medically rather than punitively. Indignation, though on the whole a useful social force, becomes harmful when it is directed against the victims of maladies that only medical skill can cure.

The same sort of thing happens as regards whole nations. During the last war, very naturally, people's vindictive feelings were aroused against the Germans, who were severely punished after their defeat. Now many people are arguing that the Versailles Treaty was ridiculously mild, since it failed to teach a lesson; this time, we are told, there must be *real* severity. To my mind, we shall be more likely to prevent a repetition of German aggression if we regard the rank and file of the Nazis as we regard lunatics than if we think of them as merely and simply criminals. Lunatics, of course, have to be restrained; we do not allow them to carry firearms. Similarly the German nation will have to be disarmed. But lunatics are restrained from prudence, not as a punishment, and so far as prudence permits we try to make them happy. Everybody recognizes that a homicidal maniac will only become more homicidal if he is made miserable. In Germany at the present day, there are, of course, many men among the Nazis who are plain criminals, but there must also be many who are more or less mad. Leaving the leaders out of account (I do not urge leniency toward them), the bulk of the German nation is much more likely to learn cooperation with the rest of the world if it is subjected to a kind but firm curative treatment than if it is regarded as an outcast among the nations. Those who are being punished seldom learn to feel kindly towards the men who punish them. And so long as the Germans hate the rest of mankind peace will be precarious.

When one reads of the beliefs of savages, or of the ancient Babylonians and Egyptians, they seem surprising by their capricious absurdity. But beliefs that are just as absurd are still entertained by the uneducated even in the most modern and civilized societies. I have been gravely assured, in America, that people born in March are unlucky and people born in May are peculiarly liable to corns. I do not know the history of these superstitions, but probably they are derived from Babylonian or Egyptian priestly lore. Beliefs begin in the higher social strata, and then, like mud in a river, sink gradually downwards in the educational scale; they may take 3,000 or 4,000 years to sink all the way. You may find your colored help making some remark that comes straight out of Plato—not the parts of Plato that scholars quote, but the parts where he utters obvious nonsense; such as that men who do not pursue wisdom in this life will be born again as women. Commentators on great philosophers always politely ignore their silly remarks.

Aristotle, in spite of his reputation, is full of absurdities. He says that children should be conceived in the Winter, when the wind is in the North, and that if people marry too young the children will be female. He tells us that the blood of females is blacker than that of males; that the pig is the only animal liable to measles; that an elephant suffering from insomnia should have its shoulders rubbed with salt, olive-oil, and warm water; that women have fewer teeth than men, and so on. Nevertheless, he is considered by the great majority of philosophers a paragon of wisdom.

Superstitions about lucky and unlucky days are almost universal. In ancient times they governed the actions of generals. Among ourselves the prejudice against Friday and the number 13 is very active; sailors do not like to sail on a Friday, and many hotels have no 13th floor. The superstitions about Friday and 13 were once believed by those reputed wise; now such men regard them as harmless follies. But probably 2,000 years hence many beliefs of the wise of our day will have come to seem equally foolish. Man is a credulous animal, and must believe *something;* in the absence of good grounds for belief, he will be satisfied with bad ones.

Belief in "nature" and what is "natural" is a source of many errors. It used to be, and to some extent still is, powerfully operative in medicine. The human body, left to itself, has a certain power of curing itself; small cuts usually heal, colds pass off, and even serious diseases sometimes disappear without medical treatment. But aids to nature are very desirable, even in these cases. Cuts may turn septic if not disinfected, colds may turn to pneumonia, and serious diseases are only left without treatment by explorers and travelers in remote regions, who have no option. Many practices which have come to seem "natural" were originally "unnatural," for instance clothing and washing. Before men adopted clothing they must have found it impossible to live in cold climates. Where there is not a modicum of cleanliness, populations suffer from various diseases, such as typhus, from which western nations have become exempt. Vaccination was (and by some still is) objected to as "unnatural." But there is no consistency in such objections, for no one supposes that a broken bone can be mended by "natural" behavior. Eating cooked food is "unnatural"; so is heating our houses. The Chinese philosopher Lao-tse, whose traditional date is about 600 B.C., objected to roads and bridges and boats as unnatural, and in his disgust at such mechanistic devices left China and went to live among the Western barbarians. Every advance in civilization has been denounced as unnatural while it was recent.

The commonest objection to birth control is that it is against "nature." (For some reason we are not allowed to say that celibacy is against nature; the only reason I can think of is that it is not new.) Malthus saw only three ways of keeping down the population; moral restraint, vice, and misery. Moral restraint, he admitted, was not likely to be practiced on a large scale. "Vice," i.e. birth control, he, as a clergyman, viewed with abhorrence. There remained misery. In his comfortable parsonage, he contemplated the misery of the great majority of mankind with equanimity, and pointed out the fallacies of reformers who hoped to alleviate it. Modern theological opponents of birth control are less honest. They pretend to think that God will provide, however many mouths there may be to feed. They ignore the fact that He has never done so hitherto, but has left mankind exposed to periodical famines in which millions died of hunger. They must be deemed to hold—if they are saying what they believe—that from this moment onwards God will work a continual miracle of loaves and fishes which He has hitherto thought unnecessary. Or perhaps they will say that suffering here below is of no importance; what matters is the hereafter. By their own theology, most of the children whom their opposition to birth conrtol will cause to exist will go to hell. We must suppose, therefore, that they oppose the amelioration of life on earth because they think it a good thing that many millions should suffer eternal torment. By comparison with them, Malthus appears merciful.

Women, as the object of our strongest love and aversion, rouse complex emotions which are embodied in proverbial "wisdom."

Almost everybody allows himself or herself some entirely unjustifiable generalization on the subject of Woman. Married men, when they generalize on that subject, judge by their wives; women judge by themselves. It would be amusing to write a history of men's views on women. In antiquity, when male supremacy was unquestioned and Christian ethics were still unknown, women were harmless but rather silly, and a man who took them seriously was somewhat despised. Plato thinks it a grave objection to the drama that the playwright has to imitate women in creating his female roles. With the coming of Christianity woman took on a new part, that of the temptress; but at the same time she was also found capable of being a saint. In Victorian days the saint was much more emphasized than the temptress; Victorian men could not admit themselves susceptible to temptation. The superior virtue of women was made a reason for keeping them out of politics, where, it was held, a lofty virtue is impossible. But the early feminists turned the argument round, and contended that the participation of women would ennoble politics. Since this has turned out to be an illusion, there has been less talk of women's superior virtue, but there are still a number of men who adhere to the monkish view of woman as the temptress. Women themselves, for the most part, think of themselves as the sensible sex, whose business it is to undo the harm that comes of men's impetuous follies. For my part I distrust *all* generalizations about women, favorable and unfavorable, masculine and feminine, ancient and modern; all alike, I should say, result from paucity of experience.

The deeply irrational attitude of each sex towards women may be seen in novels, particularly in bad novels. In bad novels by men, there is the woman with whom the author is in love, who usually possesses every charm, but is somewhat helpless, and requires male protection; sometimes, however, like Shakespeare's Cleopatra, she is an object of exasperated hatred, and is thought to be deeply and desperately wicked. In portraying the heroine, the male author does not write from observation, but merely objectifies his own emotions. In regard to his other female characters, he is more objective, and may even depend upon his notebook; but when he is in love, his passion makes a mist between him and the object of his devotion. Women novelists, also, have two kinds of women in their books. One is themselves, glamorous and kind, an object of lust to the wicked and of love to the good, sensitive, high-souled, and constantly misjudged. The other kind is represented by all other women, and is usually portrayed as petty, spiteful, cruel, and deceitful. It would seem that to judge women without bias is not easy either for men or for women.

Generalizations about national characteristics are just as common and just as unwarranted as generalizations about women. Until 1870, the Germans were thought of as a nation of spectacled professors, evolving everything out of their inner consciousness, and scarcely aware of the outer world, but since 1870 this conception has had to be very sharply revised. Frenchmen seem to be thought of by most Americans as perpetually engaged in amorous intrigue; Walt Whitman, in one of his catalogues, speaks of "the adulterous French couple on the sly settee." Americans who go to live in France are astonished, and perhaps disappointed, by the intensity of family life. Before the Russian Revolution, the Russians were credited with a mystical Slav soul, which, while it incapacitated them for ordinary sensible behavior, gave them a kind of deep wisdom to which more practical nations could not hope to attain. Suddenly everything was changed: mysticism was taboo, and only the most earthly ideals were tolerated. The truth is that what appears to one nation as the national character of another depends upon a few prominent individuals, or upon the class that happens to have power. For this reason, all generalizations on this subject are liable to be completely upset by any important political change.

To avoid the various foolish opinions to which mankind are prone, no superhuman genius is required. A few simple rules will keep you, not from *all* error, but from silly error.

If the matter is one that can be settled by observation, make the observation yourself. Aristotle could have avoided the mistake of thinking that women have fewer teeth than men, by the simple device of asking Mrs. Aristotle to keep her mouth open while he counted. He did not do so because he thought he knew. Thinking that you know when in fact you don't is a fatal mistake, to which we are all prone. I believe myself that hedgehogs eat black beetles because I have been told that they do; but if I were writing a book on the habits of hedgehogs, I should not commit myself until I had seen one enjoying this unappetizing diet. Aristotle, however, was less cautious. Ancient and medieval authors knew all about unicorns and salamanders; not one of them thought it necessary to avoid dogmatic statements about them because he had never seen one of them.

Many matters, however, are less easily brought to the test of experience. If like most of mankind, you have passionate convictions on many such matters, there are ways in which you can make yourself aware of your own bias. If an opinion contrary to your own makes you angry, that is a sign that you are subconsciously aware of having no good reason for thinking as you do. If some one maintains that two and two are five, or that Iceland is on the equator, you feel pity rather than anger, unless you know so little of arithmetic or geography that his opinion shakes your own contrary conviction. The most savage controversies are those about matters as to which there is no good evidence either way. Persecution is used in theology, not in arithmetic, because in arithmetic there is knowledge, but in theology there is only opinion. So whenever you find yourself getting angry about a difference of opinion, be on your guard; you will probably find, on examination, that your belief is going beyond what the evidence warrants.

A good way of ridding yourself of certain kinds of dogmatism is to become aware of opinions held in social circles different from your own. When I was young, I lived much outside my own country—in France, Germany, Italy, and the United States. I found this very profitable in diminishing the intensity of insular prejudice. If you cannot travel, seek out people with whom you disagree, and read a newspaper belonging to a party that is not yours. If the people and the newspaper seem mad, perverse, and wicked, remind yourself that you seem so to them.

In this opinion both parties may be right, but they cannot both be wrong. This reflection should generate a certain caution.

Becoming aware of foreign customs, however, does not always have a beneficial effect. In the 17th Century, when the Manchus conquered China, it was the custom among the Chinese for the women to have small feet, and among the Manchus for the men to wear pigtails. Instead of each dropping their own foolish custom, they each adopted the foolish custom of the other, and the Chinese continued to wear pigtails until they shook off the domination of the Manchus in the revolution of 1911.

For those who have enough psychological imagination, it is a good plan to imagine an argument with a person having a different bias. This has one advantage, and only one, as compared with actual conversation with opponents; this one advantage is that the method is not subject to the same limitations of time or space. Mahatma Gandhi deplores railways and steamboats and machinery; he would like to undo the whole of the industrial revolution. You may never have an opportunity of actually meeting any one who holds this opinion, because in Western countries most people take the advantage of modern technique for granted. But if you want to make sure that you are right in agreeing with the prevailing opinion, you will find it a good plan to test the arguments that occur to you by considering what Gandhi might say in refutation of them. I have sometimes been led actually to change my mind as a result of this kind of imaginary dialogue, and, short of this, I have frequently found myself growing less dogmatic and cocksure through realizing the possible reasonableness of a hypothetical opponent.

Be very wary of opinions that flatter your self-esteem. Both men and women, nine times out of ten, are firmly convinced of the superior excellence of their own sex. There is abundant evidence on both sides. If you are a man, you can point out that most poets and men of science are male; if you are a woman, you can retort that so are most criminals. The question is inherently insoluble, but self-esteem conceals this from most people. We are all, whatever part of the world we come from, persuaded that our own nation is superior to all others. Seeing that each nation has its characteristic merits and demerits, we adjust our standard of values so as to make out that the merits possessed by our nation are the really important ones, while its demerits are comparatively trivial. Here, again, the rational man will admit that the question is one to which there is no demonstrably right answer. It is more difficult to deal with the self-esteem of man as man, because we cannot argue out the matter with some non-human mind. The only way I know of dealing with this general human conceit is to remind ourselves that man is a brief episode in the life of a small planet in a little corner of the universe, and that, for aught we know, other parts of the cosmos may contain beings as superior to ourselves as we are to jelly-fish.

Other passions besides self-esteem are common

sources of error; of these perhaps the most important is fear. Fear sometimes operates directly, by inventing rumors of disaster in war-time, or by imagining objects of terror, such as ghosts. Sometimes it operates indirectly, by creating belief in something comforting, such as the elixir of life, or heaven for ourselves and hell for our enemies. Fear has many forms —fear of death, fear of the dark, fear of the unknown, fear of the herd, and that vague generalized fear that comes to those who conceal from themselves their more specific terrors. Until you have admitted your own fears to yourself, and have guarded yourself by a difficult effort of will against their myth-making power, you cannot hope to think truly about many matters of great importance, especially those with which religious beliefs are concerned. Fear is the main source of superstition, and one of the main sources of cruelty. To conquer fear is the beginning of wisdom, in the pursuit of truth as in the endeavor after a worthy manner of life.

There are two ways of avoiding fear: one is by persuading ourselves that we are immune from disaster, and the other is by the practice of sheer courage. The latter is difficult, and to everybody becomes impossible at a certain point. The former has therefore always been more popular. Primitive magic has the purpose of securing safety, either by injuring enemies, or by protecting oneself by talismans, spells, or incantations. Without any essential change, belief in such ways of avoiding danger survived throughout the many centuries of Babylonian civilization, spread from Babylon throughout the Empire of Alexander, and was acquired by the Romans in the course of their absorption of hellenistic culture. From the Romans it descended to medieval Christendom and Islam. Science has now lessened the belief in magic, but many people place more faith in mascots than they are willing to avow, and sorcery, while condemned by the Church, is still officially a *possible* sin.

Magic, however, was a crude way of avoiding terrors, and, moreover, not a very effective way, for wicked magicians might always prove stronger than good ones. In the 15th, 16th, and 17th centuries, dread of witches and sorcerers led to the burning of hundreds of thousands convicted of these crimes. But newer beliefs, particularly as to the future life, sought more effective ways of combating fear. Socrates on the day of his death (if Plato is to be believed) expressed the conviction that in the next world he would live in the company of the gods and heroes, and surrounded by just spirits who would never object to his endless argumentation. Plato, in his "Republic," laid it down that cheerful views of the next world must be enforced by the State, not because they were true, but to make soldiers more willing to die in battle. He would have none of the traditional myths about Hades, because they represented the spirits of the dead as unhappy.

Orthodox Christianity, in the Ages of Faith, laid down very definite rules for salvation. First, you must be baptized; then, you must avoid all theological error; last, you must, before dying, repent of your sins and receive absolution. All this would not save you from purgatory, but it would insure your ultimate arrival in heaven. It was not necessary to *know* theology. An eminent Cardinal stated authoritatively that the requirements of orthodoxy would be satisfied if you murmured on your death-bed: "I believe all that the Church believes; the Church believes all that I believe." These very definite directions ought to have made Catholics sure of finding the way to heaven. Nevertheless, the dread of hell persisted, and has caused, in recent times, a great softening of the dogmas as to who will be damned. The doctrine, professed by many modern Christians, that everybody will go to heaven, ought to do away with the fear of death, but in fact this fear is too instinctive to be easily vanquished. F. W. H. Myers, whom spiritualism had converted to belief in a future life, questioned a woman who had lately lost her daughter as to what she supposed had become of her soul. The mother replied: "Oh, well, I suppose she is enjoying eternal bliss, but I wish you wouldn't talk about such unpleasant subjects." In spite of all that theology can do, heaven remains, to most people, an "unpleasant subject."

The most refined religions, such as those of Marcus Aurelius and Spinoza, are still concerned with the conquest of fear. The Stoic doctrine was simple: it maintained that the only true good is virtue, of which no enemy can deprive me; consequently, there is no need to fear enemies. The difficulty was that no one could really believe virtue to be the only good, not even Marcus Aurelius, who, as Emperor, sought not only to make his subjects virtuous, but to protect them against barbarians, pestilences, and famines. Spinoza taught a somewhat similar doctrine. According to him, our true good consists in indifference to our mundane fortunes. Both these men sought to escape from fear by pretending that such things as physical suffering are not really evil. This is a noble way of escaping from fear, but is still based upon false belief. And if genuinely accepted, it would have the bad effect of making men indifferent, not only to their own sufferings, but also to those of others.

Under the influence of great fear, almost everybody becomes superstitious. The sailors who threw Jonah overboard imagined his presence to be the cause of the storm which threatened to wreck their ship. In a similar spirit the Japanese, at the time of the Tokio earthquake, took to massacring Koreans and Liberals. When the Romans won victories in the Punic wars, the Carthaginians became persuaded that their misfortunes were due to a certain laxity which had crept into the worship of Moloch. Moloch liked having children sacrificed to him, and preferred them aristocratic; but the noble families of Carthage had adopted the practice of surreptitiously substituting plebeian children for their own offspring. This, it was thought, had displeased the god, and at the worst moments even the most aristocratic children were duly consumed in the fire. Strange to say, the Romans were victorious in spite of this democratic reform on the part of their enemies.

Collective fear stimulates herd instinct, and tends to produce ferocity towards those who are not regarded as members of the herd. So it was in the French Revolution, when dread of foreign armies produced the reign of terror. And it is to be feared that the Nazis, as defeat draws nearer, will increase the intensity of their campaign for exterminating Jews. Fear generates impulses of cruelty, and therefore promotes such superstitious beliefs as seem to justify cruelty. Neither a man nor a crowd nor a nation can be trusted to act humanely or to think sanely under the influence of a great fear. And for this reason poltroons are more prone to cruelty than brave men, and are also more prone to superstition. When I say this, I am thinking of men who are brave in all respects, not only in facing death. Many a man will have the courage to die gallantly, but will not have the courage to say, or even to think, that the cause for which he is asked to die is an unworthy one. Obloquy is, to most men, more painful than death; that is one reason why, in times of collective excitement, so few men venture to dissent from the prevailing opinion. No Carthaginian denied Moloch, because to do so would have required more courage than was required to face death in battle.

But we have been getting too solemn. Superstitions are not always dark and cruel; often they add to the gaiety of life. I received once a communication from the god Osiris, giving me his telephone number; he lived, at that time, in a suburb of Boston. Although I did not enroll myself among his worshipers, his letter gave me pleasure. I have frequently received letters from men announcing themselves as the Messiah, and urging me not to omit to mention this important fact in my lectures. During prohibition, there was a sect which maintained that the communion service ought to be celebrated in whisky, not in wine; this tenet gave them a legal right to a supply of hard liquor, and the sect grew rapidly. There is in England a sect which maintains that the English are the lost 10 tribes; there is a stricter sect, which maintains that they are only the tribes of Ephraim and Manasseh. Whenever I encounter a member of either of these sects, I profess myself an adherent of the other, and much pleasant argumentation results. I like also the men who study the Great Pyramid, with a view to deciphering its mystical lore. Many great books have been written on this subject, some of which have been presented to me by their authors. It is a singular fact that the Great Pyramid always predicts the history of the world accurately up to the date of publication of the book in question, but after that date it becomes less reliable. Generally the author expects, very soon, wars in Egypt, followed by Armageddon and the coming of Antichrist, but by this time so many people have been recognized as Antichrist that the reader is reluctantly driven to skepticism.

I admire especially a certain prophetess who lived beside a lake in Northern New York State about the year 1820. She announced to her numerous followers that she possessed the power of walking on water, and that she proposed to do so at 11 o'clock on a certain morning. At the stated time, the faithful assembled in their thousands beside the lake. She spoke to them, saying: "Are you all entirely persuaded that I can walk on water"? With one voice they replied: "We are." "In that case," she announced, "there is not need for me to do so." And they all went home much edified.

Perhaps the world would lose some of its interest and variety if such beliefs were wholly replaced by cold science. Perhaps we may allow ourselves to be glad of the Abecedarians, who were so-called because, having rejected all profane learning, they thought it wicked to learn the ABC. And we may enjoy the perplexity of the South American Jesuit who wondered how the sloth could have traveled, since the Flood, all the way from Mount Ararat to Peru—a journey which its extreme tardiness of locomotion rendered almost incredible. A wise man will enjoy the goods of which there is a plentiful supply, and of intellectual rubbish he will find an abundant diet, in our own age as in every other.

III

ATHEISM AND AGNOSTICISM

I speak as one who was intended by my father to be brought up as a Rationalist. He was quite as much of a Rationalist as I am, but he died when I was three years old, and the Court of Chancery decided that I was to have the benefits of a Christian education.

I think that perhaps the Court of Chancery may have regretted that since. It does not seem to have done as much good as they hoped.

Perhaps you may say that it would be rather a pity if Christian education were to cease, because you would then get no more Rationalists.

They arise chiefly out of reaction to a system of education which considers it quite right that a father should decree that his son should be brought up as a Muggletonian, we will say, or brought up on any other kind of nonsense, but he must on no account be brought up to try to think rationally. When I was young that was considered to be illegal.

SIN AND THE BISHOPS

Since I became a Rationalist I have found that there is still considerable scope in the world for the practical importance of a Rationalist outlook, not only in matters of geology, but in all sorts of practical matters, such as divorce and birth control, and a question which has come up quite recently, artificial insemination, where bishops tell us that something is gravely sinful, but it is only gravely sinful because there is some text in the Bible about it. It is not gravely sinful because it does anybody harm, and that is not the argument.

As long as you can say, and as long as you can persuade Parliament to go on saying, that a thing must not be done solely because there is a text in the Bible about it, so long obviously there is great need of Rationalism in practice.

As you may know, I got into considerable trouble in the United States solely because, on some practical issues, I considered that the ethical advice given in the Bible was not conclusive, and that on some points one should act differently from what the Bible says. On that ground it was decreed by a Law Court that I was not a fit person to teach in any University in the United States, so that I have some practical ground for preferring Rationalism to other outlooks.

DON'T BE TOO CERTAIN!

The question of how to define Rationalism is not altogether an easy one. I do not think that you could define it by rejection of this or that Christian dogma. It would be perfectly possible to be a complete and absolute Rationalist in the true sense of the term and yet accept this or that dogma.

The question is how to arrive at your opinions and not what your opinions are. The thing in which we believe is the supremacy of reason. If reason should lead you to orthodox conclusions, well and good; you are still a Rationalist. To my mind the essential thing is that one should base one's arguments upon the kind of grounds that are accepted in science, and that one should not regard anything that one accepts as quite certain, but only as probable in a greater or a less degree.

Not to be absolutely certain is, I think, one of the essential things in rationality.

PROOF OF GOD

Here there comes in a practical question which has often troubled me. Whenever I go into a foreign country or a prison or any similar place they always ask me what is my religion.

I never quite know whether I should say "Agnostic" or whether I should say "Atheist." It is a very difficult question and I daresay that some of you have been troubled about it.

As a philosopher, if I were speaking to a purely philosophic audience I should say that I ought to describe myself as an Agnostic, because I do not think that there is a conclusive argument by which one can prove that there is not a God.

On the other hand, if I am to convey the right impression to the ordinary man in the street I think that

I ought to say that I am an Atheist, because when I say that I cannot prove that there is not a God, I ought to add equally that I cannot prove that there are not the Homeric gods.

None of us would seriously consider the possibility that all the gods of Homer really exist, and yet if you were to set to work to give a logical demonstration that Zeus, Hera, Poseidon, and the rest of them did not exist you would find it an awful job. You could not get such proof.

Therefore, in regard to the Olympic gods, speaking to a purely philosophic audience, I would say that I am an Agnostic. But speaking popularly, I think that all of us would say in regard to those gods that we were Atheists. In regard to the Christian God, I should, I think, take exactly the same line.

SKEPTICISM

There is exactly the same degree of possibility and likelihood of the existence of the Christian God as there is of the existence of the Homeric God. I cannot prove that either the Christian God or the Homeric gods do not exist, but I do not think that their existence is an alternative that is sufficiently probable to be worth serious consideration. Therefore, I suppose that on these documents that they submit to me on these occasions I ought to say "Atheist," although it has been a very difficult problem, and sometimes I have said one and sometimes the other without any clear principle by which to go.

When one admits that nothing is certain one must, I think, also add that some things are much more nearly certain than others. It is much more nearly certain that we are here assembled tonight than it is that this or that political party is in the right.

Certainly there are degrees of certainty, and one should be very careful to emphasize that fact, because otherwise one is landed in an utter skepticism, and complete skepticism would, of course, be totally barren and totally useless.

PERSECUTION

One must remember that some things are very much more probable than others and may be so probable that it is not worth while to remember in practice that they are not wholly certain, except when it comes to questions of persecution.

If it comes to burning somebody at the stake for not believing it, then it is worth while to remember that after all he may be right, and it is not worth while to persecute him.

In general, if a man says, for instance, that the earth is flat, I am quite willing that he should propagate his opinion as hard as he likes. He may, of course, be right but I do not think that he is. In practice you will, I think, do better to assume that the earth is round, although, of course, you may be mistaken. Therefore, I do not think that we should go in for complete skepticism, but for a doctrine of degrees of probability.

I think that, on the whole, that is the kind of doctrine that the world needs. The world has become very full of new dogmas. The old dogmas have perhaps decayed, but new dogmas have arisen and, on the whole, I think that a dogma is harmful in proportion to its novelty. New dogmas are much worse than old ones.

IV

ON BEING OLD *

There are both advantages and disadvantages in being very old. The disadvantages are obvious and uninteresting, and I shall say little about them. The advantages seem to me more interesting.

A long retrospect gives weight and substance to experience. I have been able to follow many lives, both of friends and of public characters, from an early stage to their conclusion. Some, who were promising in youth, have achieved little of value; others have continued to develop from strength to strength through long lives of important achievement. Undoubtedly, experience makes it easier to guess to which of these two kinds a young person is likely to belong.

It is not only the lives of individuals, but the lives of movements that come, with time, to form part of personal experience and to facilitate estimates of probable success or failure. Communism, in spite of a very difficult beginning, has hitherto continued to increase in power and influence. Nazism, on the contrary, by snatching too early and too ruthlessly at dominion, came to grief. To have watched such diverse processes helps to give an insight into the past of history and should help in guessing at the probable future.

* © 1962, *The Observer*, London.

EASY LABELS

To come to more personal matters. It is natural for those who are energetic and adventurous to feel in youth a very passionate and restless desire for some important achievement, without any clear prevision of what, with luck, it may be. In old age, one becomes more aware of what has, and what has not, been achieved. What one can further do becomes a smaller proportion of what has already been done, and this makes personal life less feverish.

It is a curious sensation to read the journalistic clichés which come to be fastened on past periods that one remembers, such as the "naughty nineties" and the "riotous twenties." These decades did not seem, at the time, at all "naughty" or "riotous." The habit of affixing easy labels is convenient to those who wish to seem clever without having to think, but it has very little relation to reality. The world is always changing, but not in the simple ways that such convenient clichés suggest.

Old age, as I am experiencing it, could be a time of very complete happiness if one could forget the state of the world. Privately, I enjoy everything that could make life delightful. I used to think that when I reached old age I would retire from the world and live a life of elegant culture, reading all the great books that I ought to have read at an earlier date.

Perhaps it was, in any case, an idle dream. A long habit of work with some purpose that one believes important is difficult to break, and I might have found elegant leisure boring even if the world had been in a better state. However that might have been, I find it impossible to ignore what is happening.

Ever since 1914, at almost every crucial moment, the wrong thing has been done. We are told that the West is engaged in defending the "Free World," but freedom such as existed before 1914 is now as dim a memory as crinolines. Supposedly wise men assured us in 1914 that we were fighting a war to end war, but it turned out to be a war to end peace. We were told that Prussian militarism was all that had to be put down; and, ever since, militarism has continually increased. Murderous humbug, such as would have shocked almost everyone when I was young, is now solemnly mouthed by eminent statesmen. My own country, led by men without imagination and without capacity for adaptation to the modern world, pursues a policy which, if not changed, will lead almost inevitably to the complete extermination of all the inhabitants of Britain. Like Cassandra, I am doomed to prophesy evil and not be believed. Her prophecies came true, I desperately hope that mine will not.

MORE OF A REBEL

Sometimes one is tempted to take refuge in cheerful fantasies and to imagine that perhaps in Mars or Venus happier and saner forms of life exist, but our frantic skill is making this a vain dream. Before long, if we do not destroy ourselves, our destructive strife will have spread to those planets. Perhaps, for their sake, one ought to hope that war on earth will put an end to our species before its folly has become cosmic. But this is not a hope in which I can find any comfort.

The way in which the world has developed during the last 50 years has brought about in me changes opposite to those which are supposed to be typical of old age. One is frequently assured by men who have no doubt of their own wisdom that old age should bring serenity and a larger vision in which seeming evils are viewed as means to ultimate good.

I cannot accept any such view. Serenity, in the present world, can only be achieved through blindness or brutality. Unlike what is conventionally expected, I become gradually more and more of a rebel. I was not born rebellious. Until 1914, I fitted more or less comfortably into the world as I found it. There were evils—great evils—but there was reason to think that they would grow less. Without having the temperament of a rebel, the course of events has made me gradually less and less able to acquiesce patiently in what is happening. A minority, though a growing one, feels as I do, and so long as I live, it is with them that I must work.